God's Light™ *on Praise & Worship*

Requests for information should be addressed t

ZondervanPublishingHouse
Mail Drop B20
Grand Rapids, Michigan 49530
http://www.zondervan.com

Developed and produced by The Livin
tion

oject staff: Christopher D. Hudson
msted, Carol Smith

dervan editorial and design: Car
uwkamp, Sarah Hupp, Sherri L.

N 0-310-97426-7

00 01 02 03 04 05 06 07/HK

For

____

Praise the LORD. Give thanks to the LORD, for he is good; his love endures forever.

—*Psalm 106:1*

From

____

GOD'S LIGHT™

ON PRAISE & WORSHIP

COMPILED BY DAWN M. OLMSTED

CONTENTS

A Blueprint for Worship

The Participants in Praise & Worship........9
The Time for Praise & Worship 15
The Tools for Praise & Worship 17
The Focus for Praise & Worship.............25

Worship God for Who He Is

Ever Loving...31
All Wise 34
Always Faithful..38
Strong & Powerful...................................42
Great & Awesome....................................48
Merciful & Gracious...............................54
Holy & Just...57
Glorious Sovereign 63
Forgiving Redeemer................................66

Worship God for What He Has Done

Answered Prayer......................................77
Blessings...80
Comfort & Consolation..........................87
Creation 92
Guidance..97
Peace 99

Presence of the Holy Spirit 103
Protection & Provision 106
Salvation 111

A Simple Way of Worshiping

Praising God's Very Nature 119
Celebrating God's Goodness 122
Worshiping Together 125
Exalting God..127
God is with Us 130
Jesus' Example 134

Examples of Worship

Angels 139
Daniel..143
David...144
Deborah & Barak 146
Hannah 149
Mary..150
Moses..152
Simeon 154
Solomon..156
Zechariah 159

A Blueprint for *Worship*

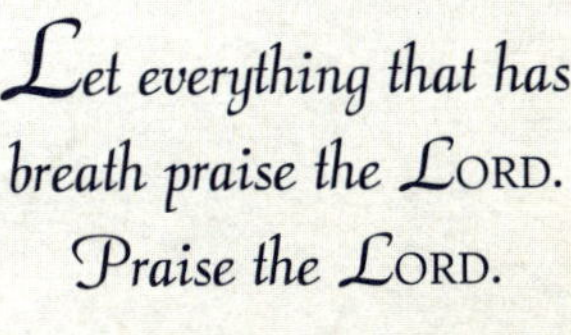

Let everything that has breath praise the Lord. *Praise the* Lord.

—Psalm 150:6

The Participants in Praise & Worship

Praise the LORD from the earth, you great sea creatures and all ocean depths, lightning and hail, snow and clouds, stormy winds that do his bidding, you mountains and all hills, fruit trees and all cedars, wild animals and all cattle, small creatures and flying birds, kings of the earth and all nations, you princes and all rulers on earth, young men and maidens, old men and children. Let them praise the name of the LORD.

—*Psalm 148:7-13*

The heavens declare the glory of God; the skies proclaim the work of his hands.

—*Psalm 19:1*

Sing for joy, O heavens, for the LORD has done this; shout aloud, O earth beneath. Burst into song, you mountains, you forests and all your trees, for the LORD has redeemed Jacob, he displays his glory in Israel.

—*Isaiah 44:23*

Let the heavens rejoice, let the earth be glad; let the sea resound, and all that is in it; let the fields be jubilant, and everything in them. Then all the trees of the forest will sing for joy; they will sing before the LORD.

—*Psalm 96:11-13*

Sing to the LORD a new song, his praise from the ends of the earth, you who go down to the sea, and all that is in it, you islands, and all who live in them.

—*Isaiah 42:10*

Shout for joy to the LORD, all the earth, burst into jubilant song with music.

—*Psalm 98:4*

I heard every creature in heaven and on earth and under the earth and on the sea, and all that is in them, singing: "To him who sits on the throne and to the Lamb be praise and honor and glory and power, for ever and ever!"

—*Revelation 5:13*

Shout for joy, O heavens; rejoice, O earth; burst into song, O mountains! For the LORD comforts his people and will have compassion on his afflicted ones.

—*Isaiah 49:13*

Praise the LORD, all his works everywhere in his dominion. Praise the LORD, O my soul.

—*Psalm 103:22*

The LORD is good to all; he has compassion on all he has made. All you have made will praise you, O LORD; your saints will extol you.

—*Psalm 145:9-10*

The trumpeters and singers joined in unison, as with one voice, to give praise and thanks to the LORD.

—*2 Chronicles 5:13*

Praise the LORD. Sing to the LORD a new song, his praise in the assembly of the saints.

—*Psalm 149:1*

The great crowd that had come for the Feast heard that Jesus was on his way to Jerusalem. They took palm branches and went out to meet him, shouting, "Hosanna!" "Blessed is he who comes in the name of the Lord!" "Blessed is the King of Israel!"

—*John 12:12-13*

I will give you thanks in the great assembly; among throngs of people I will praise you.

—*Psalm 35:18*

David said to the whole assembly, "Praise the LORD your God." So they all praised the LORD, the God of their fathers; they bowed low and fell prostrate before the LORD and the king.

—*1 Chronicles 29:20*

The Levites—Jeshua, Kadmiel, Bani, Hashabneiah, Sherebiah, Hodiah, Shebaniah and Pethahiah—said: "Stand up and praise the LORD your God, who is from everlasting to everlasting." "Blessed be your glorious name, and may it be exalted above all blessing and praise. You alone are the LORD. You made the heavens, even the highest heavens, and all their starry host, the earth and all that is on it, the seas and all that is in them. You give life to everything, and the multitudes of heaven worship you."

—*Nehemiah 9:5-6*

The Time for Praise & Worship

I will extol the LORD at all times; his praise will always be on my lips.

—Psalm 34:1

This is the day the LORD has made; let us rejoice and be glad in it.

—Psalm 118:24

When you have eaten and are satisfied, praise the LORD your God for the good land he has given you.

—Deuteronomy 8:10

Praise the LORD. I will extol the LORD with all my heart in the council of the upright and in the assembly.

—Psalm 111:1

Every day I will praise you and extol your name for ever and ever.

—*Psalm 145:2*

When I am afraid, I will trust in you. In God, whose word I praise, in God I trust; I will not be afraid. What can mortal man do to me?

—*Psalm 56:3-4*

The people were amazed when they saw the mute speaking, the crippled made well, the lame walking and the blind seeing. And they praised the God of Israel.

—*Matthew 15:31*

Sing to the LORD, praise his name; proclaim his salvation day after day.

—*Psalm 96:2*

The Tools for Praise & Worship

I will praise you, O LORD, among the nations; I will sing praises to your name.

—*2 Samuel 22:50*

Praise the LORD. Praise God in his sanctuary; praise him in his mighty heavens. Praise him for his acts of power; praise him for his surpassing greatness. Praise him with the sounding of the trumpet, praise him with the harp and lyre, praise him with tambourine and dancing, praise him with the strings and flute, praise him with the clash of cymbals, praise him with resounding cymbals. Let everything that has breath praise the LORD. Praise the LORD.

—*Psalm 150:1-6*

Who may ascend the hill of the LORD? Who may stand in his holy place? He who has clean hands and a pure heart, who does not lift up his soul to an idol or swear by what is false.

—*Psalm 24:3-4*

A time is coming and has now come when the true worshipers will worship the Father in spirit and truth, for they are the kind of worshipers the Father seeks. God is spirit, and his worshipers must worship in spirit and in truth.

—*John 4:23-24*

Come, let us sing for joy to the LORD; let us shout aloud to the Rock of our salvation. Let us come before him with thanksgiving and extol him with music and song.

—Psalm 95:1-2

Sing to the LORD, all the earth; proclaim his salvation day after day. Declare his glory among the nations, his marvelous deeds among all peoples.

—1 Chronicles 16:23-24

Sing joyfully to the LORD, you righteous; it is fitting for the upright to praise him.

—Psalm 33:1

You make me glad by your deeds, O LORD; I sing for joy at the works of your hands.

—Psalm 92:4

Speak to one another with psalms, hymns and spiritual songs. Sing and make music in your heart to the Lord, always giving thanks to God the Father for everything, in the name of our Lord Jesus Christ.

—*Ephesians 5:19-20*

My soul will be satisfied as with the richest of foods; with singing lips my mouth will praise you.

—*Psalm 63:5*

At the dedication of the wall of Jerusalem, the Levites were sought out from where they lived and were brought to Jerusalem to celebrate joyfully the dedication with songs of thanksgiving and with the music of cymbals, harps and lyres.

—*Nehemiah 12:27*

I will praise you with the harp for your faithfulness, O my God; I will sing praise to you with the lyre, O Holy One of Israel.

—Psalm 71:22

Sing for joy to God our strength; shout aloud to the God of Jacob! Begin the music, strike the tambourine, play the melodious harp and lyre.

—Psalm 81:1-2

It is good to praise the LORD and make music to your name, O Most High, to proclaim your love in the morning and your faithfulness at night, to the music of the ten-stringed lyre and the melody of the harp.

—Psalm 92:1-3

Awake, harp and lyre! I will awaken the dawn. I will praise you, O LORD, among the nations; I will sing of you among the peoples.

—*Psalm 108:2-3*

Sing to the LORD with thanksgiving; make music to our God on the harp.

—*Psalm 147:7*

Let them praise his name with dancing and make music to him with tambourine and harp. For the LORD takes delight in his people; he crowns the humble with salvation.

—*Psalm 149:3-4*

My heart is steadfast, O God; I will sing and make music with all my soul.

—*Psalm 108:1*

The LORD will save me, and we will sing with stringed instruments all the days of our lives in the temple of the LORD.

—*Isaiah 38:20*

I lift up my hands to your commands, which I love, and I meditate on your decrees.

—*Psalm 119:48*

Praise the LORD with the harp; make music to him on the ten-stringed lyre. Sing to him a new song; play skillfully, and shout for joy. For the word of the LORD is right and true; he is faithful in all he does.

—*Psalm 33:2-4*

Lift up your hands in the sanctuary and praise the LORD.

—*Psalm 134:2*

Let us examine our ways and test them, and let us return to the LORD. Let us lift up our hearts and our hands to God in heaven.

—*Lamentations 3:40-41*

Because your love is better than life, my lips will glorify you. I will praise you as long as I live, and in your name I will lift up my hands.

—*Psalm 63:3-4*

Shout for joy to the LORD, all the earth. Worship the LORD with gladness; come before him with joyful songs.

—*Psalm 100:1-2*

The Focus for Praise & Worship

It is written: "Worship the Lord your God and serve him only."

—Luke 4:8

Let them know that you, whose name is the LORD—that you alone are the Most High over all the earth.

—Psalm 83:18

His pleasure is not in the strength of the horse, nor his delight in the legs of a man; the LORD delights in those who fear him, who put their hope in his unfailing love. Extol the LORD.

—Psalm 147:10-12

Fear the LORD your God and serve him. Hold fast to him and take your oaths in his name. He is your praise; he is your God.

—Deuteronomy 10:20-21

I desire mercy, not sacrifice, and acknowledgment of God rather than burnt offerings.

—Hosea 6:6

Observe my Sabbaths and have reverence for my sanctuary. I am the LORD.

—Leviticus 26:2

Let all the earth fear the LORD; let all the people of the world revere him.

—Psalm 33:8

Since we are receiving a kingdom that cannot be shaken, let us be thankful, and so worship God acceptably with reverence and awe.

—Hebrews 12:28

You must always be careful to keep the decrees and ordinances, the laws and commands he wrote for you. Do not worship other gods. Do not forget the covenant I have made with you, and do not worship other gods. Rather, worship the LORD your God; it is he who will deliver you from the hand of all your enemies.

—2 Kings 17:37-39

Worship *God* for Who He Is

Holy, holy, holy is the Lord God Almighty, who was, and is, and is to come.

—Revelation 4:8

Ever Loving

Love comes from God. Everyone who loves has been born of God and knows God.

—*1 John 4:7*

I trust in the LORD. I will be glad and rejoice in your love, for you saw my affliction and knew the anguish of my soul.

—*Psalm 31:6-7*

This is how God showed his love among us: He sent his one and only Son into the world that we might live through him. This is love: not that we loved God, but that he loved us and sent his Son as an atoning sacrifice for our sins.

—*1 John 4:9-10*

You are forgiving and good, O LORD, abounding in love to all who call to you.

—Psalm 86:5

Your love, O LORD, reaches to the heavens, your faithfulness to the skies. How priceless is your unfailing love!

—Psalm 36:5,7

I pray that you, being rooted and established in love, may have power, together with all the saints, to grasp how wide and long and high and deep is the love of Christ.

—Ephesians 3:17-18

I will praise you, O LORD, among the nations; I will sing of you among the peoples. For great is your love, reaching to the heavens; your faithfulness reaches to the skies.

—*Psalm 57:9-10*

The LORD loves righteousness and justice; the earth is full of his unfailing love.

—*Psalm 33:5*

Live a life of love, just as Christ loved us and gave himself up for us as a fragrant offering and sacrifice to God.

—*Ephesians 5:2*

Praise be to God, who has not rejected my prayer or withheld his love from me!

—*Psalm 66:20*

All Wise

To God belong wisdom and power; counsel and understanding are his.

—*Job 12:13*

"My thoughts are not your thoughts, neither are your ways my ways," declares the Lord. "As the heavens are higher than the earth, so are my ways higher than your ways and my thoughts than your thoughts."

—*Isaiah 55:8-9*

How can a mortal be righteous before God? Though one wished to dispute with him, he could not answer him one time out of a thousand. His wisdom is profound, his power is vast.

—*Job 9:2-4*

The LORD gives wisdom, and from his mouth come knowledge and understanding.

—*Proverbs 2:6*

How many are your works, O LORD! In wisdom you made them all; the earth is full of your creatures.

—*Psalm 104:24*

Oh, the depth of the riches of the wisdom and knowledge of God! How unsearchable his judgments, and his paths beyond tracing out!

—*Romans 11:33*

Daniel praised the God of heaven and said: Praise be to the name of God for ever and ever; wisdom and power are his.

—*Daniel 2:19-20*

Where is the wise man? Where is the scholar? Where is the philosopher of this age? Has not God made foolish the wisdom of the world? For since in the wisdom of God the world through its wisdom did not know him, God was pleased through the foolishness of what was preached to save those who believe. For the foolishness of God is wiser than man's wisdom, and the weakness of God is stronger than man's strength.

—*1 Corinthians 1:20-21,25*

God made the earth by his power; he founded the world by his wisdom and stretched out the heavens by his understanding.

—*Jeremiah 10:12*

Where then does wisdom come from? Where does understanding dwell? It is hidden from the eyes of every living thing, concealed even from the birds of the air. God understands the way to it and he alone knows where it dwells.

—Job 28:20-21, 23

Always Faithful

Know therefore that the LORD your God is God; he is the faithful God, keeping his covenant of love to a thousand generations of those who love him and keep his commands.

—*Deuteronomy 7:9*

I will proclaim the name of the LORD. Oh, praise the greatness of our God! He is the Rock, his works are perfect, and all his ways are just. A faithful God who does no wrong, upright and just is he.

—*Deuteronomy 32:3-4*

God is faithful; he will not let you be tempted beyond what you can bear.

—*1 Corinthians 10:13*

I will praise you, O LORD, among the nations; I will sing of you among the peoples. For great is your love, reaching to the heavens; your faithfulness reaches to the skies.

—Psalm 57:9-10

Because of the LORD's great love we are not consumed, for his compassions never fail. They are new every morning; great is your faithfulness.

—Lamentations 3:22-23

The LORD is gracious and compassionate. The works of his hands are faithful and just; all his precepts are trustworthy. They are steadfast for ever and ever, done in faithfulness and uprightness.

—Psalm 111:4,7-8

O Lord, you are my God; I will exalt you and praise your name, for in perfect faithfulness you have done marvelous things, things planned long ago.

—*Isaiah 25:1*

The Lord is faithful to all his promises and loving toward all he has made.

—*Psalm 145:13*

The Lord is faithful, and he will strengthen and protect you from the evil one.

—*2 Thessalonians 3:3*

The one who calls you is faithful and he will do it.

—*1 Thessalonians 5:24*

God, who has called you into fellowship with his Son Jesus Christ our Lord, is faithful.

—*1 Corinthians 1:9*

You, O LORD, are a compassionate and gracious God, slow to anger, abounding in love and faithfulness.

—*Psalm 86:15*

Strong & Powerful

The LORD is my strength and my song; he has become my salvation. He is my God, and I will praise him, my father's God, and I will exalt him.

—Exodus 15:2

I love you, O LORD, my strength. The LORD is my rock, my fortress and my deliverer; my God is my rock, in whom I take refuge. He is my shield and the horn of my salvation, my stronghold.

—Psalm 18:1-2

In your unfailing love you will lead the people you have redeemed. In your strength you will guide them to your holy dwelling.

—Exodus 15:13

Who is God besides the LORD? And who is the Rock except our God? It is God who arms me with strength and makes my way perfect.

—*2 Samuel 22:32-33*

Proclaim the power of God, whose majesty is over Israel, whose power is in the skies.

—*Psalm 68:34*

I heard what sounded like the roar of a great multitude in heaven shouting: "Hallelujah! Salvation and glory and power belong to our God."

—*Revelation 19:1*

The LORD is the strength of his people, a fortress of salvation for his anointed one.

—*Psalm 28:8*

Surely God is my salvation; I will trust and not be afraid. The LORD, the LORD, is my strength and my song; he has become my salvation.

—*Isaiah 12:2*

God is our refuge and strength, an ever-present help in trouble.

—*Psalm 46:1*

O my Strength, I sing praise to you; you, O God, are my fortress, my loving God.

—*Psalm 59:17*

One thing God has spoken, two things have I heard: that you, O God, are strong, and that you, O LORD, are loving.

—*Psalm 62:11-12*

May God arise, may his enemies be scattered; may his foes flee before him.
As smoke is blown away by the wind, may you blow them away;
as wax melts before the fire, may the wicked perish before God.
But may the righteous be glad and rejoice before God; may they be happy and joyful.

Sing to God, sing praise to his name, extol him who rides on the clouds—his name is the Lord— and rejoice before him.
A father to the fatherless, a defender of widows, is God in his holy dwelling.
God sets the lonely in families, he leads forth the prisoners with singing; but the rebellious live in a sun-scorched land.

When you went out before your people, O God, when you marched through the wasteland,
the earth shook, the heavens poured down rain,
before God, the One of Sinai, before God, the God of Israel.
You gave abundant showers, O God; you refreshed your weary inheritance.
Your people settled in it, and from your bounty, O God, you provided for the poor.

The Lord announced the word, and great was the company of those who proclaimed it:
"Kings and armies flee in haste; in the camps men divide and plunder.
Even while you sleep among the campfires, the wings of my dove

are sheathed with silver, its feathers with shining gold."
When the Almighty scattered the kings in the land, it was like snow fallen on Zalmon.

Sing to God, O kingdom of the earth, sing praise to the Lord,
to him who rides the ancient skies above, who thunders with mighty voice.
Proclaim the power of God, whose majesty is over Israel, whose power is in the skies.
You are awesome, O God, in your sanctuary; the God of Israel gives power and strength to his people.
Praise be to God!

—*Psalm 68:1-14; 32-35*

Great & Awesome

How awesome is the LORD Most High, the great King over all the earth!

—*Psalm 47:2*

Dominion and awe belong to God; he establishes order in the heights of heaven.

—*Job 25:2*

For the LORD your God is God of gods and Lord of lords, the great God, mighty and awesome, who shows no partiality.

—*Deuteronomy 10:17*

No one is like you, O LORD; you are great, and your name is mighty in power.

—Jeremiah 10:6

Out of the north he comes in golden splendor; God comes in awesome majesty. The Almighty is beyond our reach and exalted in power; in his justice and great righteousness, he does not oppress.

—Job 37:22-23

Do not be terrified by [your enemies], for the LORD your God, who is among you, is a great and awesome God.

—Deuteronomy 7:21

Who among the gods is like you, O Lord? Who is like you—majestic in holiness, awesome in glory, working wonders?

—Exodus 15:11

Yours, O Lord, is the greatness and the power and the glory and the majesty and the splendor, for everything in heaven and earth is yours. Yours, O Lord, is the kingdom; you are exalted as head over all.

—1 Chronicles 29:11

Praise the Lord. Praise God in his sanctuary; praise him in his mighty heavens. Praise him for his acts of power; praise him for his surpassing greatness.

—Psalm 150:1-2

Great is the LORD and most worthy of praise; his greatness no one can fathom.

—*Psalm 145:3*

O LORD, God of heaven, the great and awesome God, who keeps his covenant of love with those who love him and obey his commands, let your ear be attentive and your eyes open to hear the prayer your servant is praying before you.

—*Nehemiah 1:5-6*

You are great and do marvelous deeds; you alone are God.

—*Psalm 86:10*

Sing to the LORD a new song; sing to the LORD, all the earth.

Sing to the LORD, praise his name; proclaim his salvation day after day.

Declare his glory among the nations, his marvelous deeds among all peoples.

For great is the LORD and most worthy of praise; he is to be feared above all the gods.

For all the gods of the nations are idols, but the LORD made the heavens.

Splendor and majesty are before him; strength and glory are in his sanctuary.

Ascribe to the LORD, O families of the nations, ascribe to the LORD glory and strength.

Ascribe to the LORD the glory due his name; bring an offering and come into his courts.

Worship the LORD with the splendor of his holiness; tremble before him, all the earth.

Say among the nations, "The Lord reigns." The world is firmly established, it cannot be moved; he will judge the peoples with equity.

Let the heavens rejoice, let the earth be glad; let the sea resound, and all that is in it; let the fields be jubilant, and everything in them.

Then all the trees of the forest will sing for joy; they will sing before the LORD, for he comes, he comes to judge the earth.

He will judge the world in righteousness and the peoples in his truth.

—Psalm 96:1-9

Merciful & Gracious

The Mighty One has done great things for me—holy is his name. His mercy extends to those who fear him, from generation to generation.

—Luke 1:49-50

Because of his great love for us, God, who is rich in mercy, made us alive with Christ even when we were dead in transgressions—it is by grace you have been saved.

—Ephesians 2:4-5

When the kindness and love of God our Savior appeared, he saved us, not because of righteous things we had done, but because of his mercy.

—Titus 3:4-5

Praise be to the God and Father of our Lord Jesus Christ! In his great mercy he has given us new birth into a living hope through the resurrection of Jesus Christ from the dead.

—1 Peter 1:3

All have sinned and fall short of the glory of God, and are justified freely by his grace through the redemption that came by Christ Jesus.

—Romans 3:23-24

LORD, I have heard of your fame; I stand in awe of your deeds, O LORD. Renew them in our day, in our time make them known; in wrath remember mercy.

—Habakkuk 3:2

Praise be to the LORD, for he has heard my cry for mercy. The LORD is my strength and my shield; my heart trusts in him, and I am helped. My heart leaps for joy and I will give thanks to him in song.

—*Psalm 28:6-7*

Holy & Just

Give thanks to the LORD, for he is good; his love endures forever.

—*1 Chronicles 16:34*

I will give thanks to the LORD because of his righteousness and will sing praise to the name of the LORD Most High.

—*Psalm 7:17*

How great is your goodness, which you have stored up for those who fear you.

—*Psalm 31:19*

The LORD Almighty will be exalted by his justice, and the holy God will show himself holy by his righteousness.

—Isaiah 5:16

I will praise you, O LORD, with all my heart; I will tell of all your wonders. I will be glad and rejoice in you; I will sing praise to your name, O Most High. For you have upheld my right and my cause; you have sat on your throne, judging righteously.

—Psalm 9:1-2, 4

The LORD is righteous, he loves justice; upright men will see his face.

—Psalm 11:7

Sing to the LORD! Give praise to the LORD! He rescues the life of the needy from the hands of the wicked.

—Jeremiah 20:13

I will sing of your love and justice;
to you, O LORD, I will sing praise.

—Psalm 101:1

The LORD longs to be gracious to you; he rises to show you compassion. For the LORD is a God of justice. Blessed are all who wait for him!

—Isaiah 30:18

The LORD said: "Listen to me, my people; hear me, my nation: The law will go out from me; my justice will become a light to the nations. My righteousness draws near speedily, my salvation is on the way, and my arm will bring justice to the nations. The islands will look to me and wait in hope for my arm."

—Isaiah 51:4-5

Will not God bring about justice for his chosen ones, who cry out to him day and night? Will he keep putting them off? I tell you, he will see that they get justice, and quickly.

—*Luke 18:7-8*

You hear, O LORD, the desire of the afflicted; you encourage them, and you listen to their cry, defending the fatherless and the oppressed.

—*Psalm 10:17-18*

Who will not fear you, O Lord, and bring glory to your name? For you alone are holy. All nations will come and worship before you, for your righteous acts have been revealed.

—*Revelation 15:4*

There is no one holy like the LORD; there is no one besides you; there is no Rock like our God.

—1 Samuel 2:2

Ascribe to the LORD the glory due his name; worship the LORD in the splendor of his holiness.

—Psalm 29:2

Let the sea resound, and everything in it, the world, and all who live in it. Let the rivers clap their hands, let the mountains sing together for joy; let them sing before the LORD, for he comes to judge the earth. He will judge the world in righteousness and the peoples with equity.

—Psalm 98:7-9

One generation will commend your works to another; they will tell of your mighty acts. They will celebrate your abundant goodness and joyfully sing of your righteousness.

—*Psalm 145:4,7*

Glorious Sovereign

Yours, O LORD, is the greatness and the power and the glory and the majesty and the splendor, for everything in heaven and earth is yours. Yours, O LORD, is the kingdom; you are exalted as head over all. Wealth and honor come from you; you are the ruler of all things. In your hands are strength and power to exalt and give strength to all. Now, our God, we give you thanks, and praise your glorious name.

—1 Chronicles 29:11-13

The earth will be filled with the knowledge of the glory of the LORD, as the waters cover the sea.

—Habakkuk 2:14

The LORD reigns, he is robed in majesty; the LORD is robed in majesty and is armed with strength. The world is firmly established; it cannot be moved. Your throne was established long ago; you are from all eternity.

—*Psalm 93:1-2*

Who among the gods is like you, O LORD? Who is like you—majestic in holiness, awesome in glory, working wonders?

—*Exodus 15:11*

Splendor and majesty are before the LORD; strength and joy in his dwelling place.

—*1 Chronicles 16:27*

May they sing of the ways of the LORD, for the glory of the LORD is great.

—*Psalm 138:5*

I will exalt you, my God the King; I will praise your name for ever and ever. Every day I will praise you and extol your name for ever and ever.

—*Psalm 145:1-2*

Forgiving Redeemer

Our Redeemer—the LORD Almighty is his name—is the Holy One of Israel.

—Isaiah 47:4

I know that my Redeemer lives, and that in the end he will stand upon the earth.

—Job 19:25

He provided redemption for his people; he ordained his covenant forever—holy and awesome is his name.

—Psalm 111:9

They remembered that God was their Rock, that God Most High was their Redeemer.

—Psalm 78:35

Praise the LORD, O my soul; all my inmost being, praise his holy name. Praise the LORD, O my soul, and forget not all his benefits—who forgives all your sins and heals all your diseases.

—*Psalm 103:1-3*

Who is a God like you, who pardons sin and forgives the transgression of the remnant of his inheritance? You do not stay angry forever but delight to show mercy. You will again have compassion on us; you will tread our sins underfoot and hurl all our iniquities into the depths of the sea.

—*Micah 7:18-19*

If you return to the Almighty, you will be restored: If you remove wickedness far from your tent. Surely then you will find delight in the Almighty and will lift up your face to God. You will pray to him, and he will hear you.

—*Job 22:23,26-27*

If my people, who are called by my name, will humble themselves and pray and seek my face and turn from their wicked ways, then will I hear from heaven and will forgive their sin and will heal their land.

—*2 Chronicles 7:14*

If we confess our sins, he is faithful and just and will forgive us our sins and purify us from all unrighteousness.

—*1 John 1:9*

This is what the LORD says—Israel's King and Redeemer, the LORD Almighty: I am the first and I am the last; apart from me there is no God.

—Isaiah 44:6

He redeemed my soul from going down to the pit, and I will live to enjoy the light.

—Job 33:28

O Israel, put your hope in the LORD, for with the LORD is unfailing love and with him is full redemption.

—Psalm 130:7

This is what the LORD says—your Redeemer, who formed you in the womb: I am the LORD, who has made all things, who alone stretched out the heavens, who spread out the earth by myself.

—*Isaiah 44:24*

Give thanks to the LORD, for he is good; his love endures forever. Let the redeemed of the LORD say this.

—*Psalm 107:1-2*

Christ redeemed us from the curse of the law by becoming a curse for us, for it is written: "Cursed is everyone who is hung on a tree." He redeemed us in order that the blessing given to Abraham might come to the Gentiles through Christ Jesus, so that by faith we might receive the promise of the Spirit.

—*Galatians 3:13-14*

My lips will shout for joy when I sing praise to you—I, whom you have redeemed.

—Psalm 71:23

You know that it was not with perishable things such as silver or gold that you were redeemed from the empty way of life handed down to you from your forefathers, but with the precious blood of Christ, a lamb without blemish or defect. He was chosen before the creation of the world, but was revealed in these last times for your sake. Through him you believe in God, who raised him from the dead and glorified him, and so your faith and hope are in God.

—1 Peter 1:18-21

Praise be to the Lord, the God of Israel, because he has come and has redeemed his people.

—*Luke 1:68*

God chose us in him before the creation of the world to be holy and blameless in his sight. In love he predestined us to be adopted as his sons through Jesus Christ, in accordance with his pleasure and will—to the praise of his glorious grace, which he has freely given us in the One he loves. In him we have redemption through his blood, the forgiveness of sins, in accordance with the riches of God's grace.

—*Ephesians 1:4-7*

He has rescued us from the dominion of darkness and brought us into the kingdom of the Son he loves, in whom we have redemption, the forgiveness of sins.

—*Colossians 1:13-14*

Worship *God* for What He Has Done

He restores my soul. He guides me in paths of righteousness for his name's sake.

—Psalm 23:3

Answered Prayer

Give thanks to the LORD, call on his name; make known among the nations what he has done, and proclaim that his name is exalted. Sing to the LORD, for he has done glorious things; let this be known to all the world.

—*Isaiah 12:4-5*

Daniel praised the God of heaven and said: "I thank and praise you, O God of my fathers: You have given me wisdom and power, you have made known to me what we asked of you, you have made known to us the dream of the king."

—*Daniel 2:19,23*

Praise be to the LORD, who has given rest to his people Israel just as he promised. Not one word has failed of all the good promises he gave through his servant Moses.

—*1 Kings 8:56*

God has surely listened and heard my voice in prayer. Praise be to God, who has not rejected my prayer or withheld his love from me!

—*Psalm 66:19-20*

We cried out to the LORD, the God of our fathers, and the LORD heard our voice and saw our misery, toil and oppression. So the LORD brought us out of Egypt with a mighty hand and an outstretched arm, with great terror and with miraculous signs and wonders.

—*Deuteronomy 26:7-8*

The LORD is my strength and my shield; my heart trusts in him, and I am helped. My heart leaps for joy and I will give thanks to him in song.

—Psalm 28:7

In my distress I called to the LORD; I called out to my God. From his temple he heard my voice; my cry came to his ears.

—2 Samuel 22:7

The LORD has heard my cry for mercy; the LORD accepts my prayer.

—Psalm 6:9

Blessings

Surely, O LORD, you bless the righteous; you surround them with your favor as with a shield.

—*Psalm 5:12*

You turned my wailing into dancing; you removed my sackcloth and clothed me with joy, that my heart may sing to you and not be silent. O LORD my God, I will give you thanks forever.

—*Psalm 30:11-12*

You have made known to me the path of life; you will fill me with joy in your presence, with eternal pleasures at your right hand.

—*Psalm 16:11*

Praise be to the LORD, to God our Savior, who daily bears our burdens.

—*Psalm 68:19*

Sing to the LORD! Give praise to the LORD! He rescues the life of the needy from the hands of the wicked.

—*Jeremiah 20:13*

I will extol the LORD at all times; his praise will always be on my lips. My soul will boast in the LORD; let the afflicted hear and rejoice. Glorify the LORD with me; let us exalt his name together. I sought the LORD, and he answered me; he delivered me from all my fears.

—*Psalm 34:1-4*

I love the LORD, for he heard my voice; he heard my cry for mercy. Because he turned his ear to me, I will call on him as long as I live. The cords of death entangled me, the anguish of the grave came upon me; I was overcome by trouble and sorrow. Then I called on the name of the LORD: "O LORD, save me!" The LORD is gracious and righteous; our God is full of compassion. The LORD protects the simplehearted; when I was in great need, he saved me. Be at rest once more, O my soul, for the LORD has been good to you.

—Psalm 116:1-7

Surely you have granted [me] eternal blessings and made [me] glad with the joy of your presence.

—Psalm 21:6

I waited patiently for the LORD; he turned to me and heard my cry. He lifted me out of the slimy pit, out of the mud and mire; he set my feet on a rock and gave me a firm place to stand. He put a new song in my mouth, a hymn of praise to our God.

—*Psalm 40:1-3*

O Sovereign LORD, you are God! Your words are trustworthy, and you have promised these good things to your servant. Now be pleased to bless the house of your servant, that it may continue forever in your sight; for you, O Sovereign LORD, have spoken, and with your blessing the house of your servant will be blessed forever.

—*2 Samuel 7:28-29*

The LORD remembers us and will bless us: He will bless the house of Israel, he will bless the house of Aaron, he will bless those who fear the LORD—small and great alike.

—*Psalm 115:12-13*

In the presence of the LORD your God, you and your families shall eat and shall rejoice in everything you have put your hand to, because the LORD your God has blessed you.

—*Deuteronomy 12:7*

I trust in your unfailing love; my heart rejoices in your salvation. I will sing to the LORD, for he has been good to me.

—*Psalm 13:5-6*

Blessed are you, O Israel! Who is like you, a people saved by the LORD? He is your shield and helper and your glorious sword. Your enemies will cower before you, and you will trample down their high places.

—*Deuteronomy 33:29*

Praise the LORD, O my soul, and forget not all his benefits—who forgives all your sins and heals all your diseases, who redeems your life from the pit and crowns you with love and compassion, who satisfies your desires with good things so that your youth is renewed like the eagle's.

—*Psalm 103:2-5*

O LORD my God, I called to you for help and you healed me.

—*Psalm 30:2*

They cried to the LORD in their trouble, and he saved them from their distress. He sent forth his word and healed them; he rescued them from the grave. Let them give thanks to the LORD for his unfailing love and his wonderful deeds.

—Psalm 107:19-21

He heals the brokenhearted and binds up their wounds.

—Psalm 147:3

Comfort & Consolation

This is what the LORD says: "As a mother comforts her child, so will I comfort you."

—*Isaiah 66:13*

The ransomed of the LORD will return. They will enter Zion with singing; everlasting joy will crown their heads. Gladness and joy will overtake them, and sorrow and sighing will flee away. I, even I, am he who comforts you.

—*Isaiah 51:11-12*

When I said, "My foot is slipping," your love, O LORD, supported me. When anxiety was great within me, your consolation brought joy to my soul.

—*Psalm 94:18-19*

Jesus said: "Come to me, all you who are weary and burdened, and I will give you rest."

—*Matthew 11:28*

Those who sow in tears will reap with songs of joy.

—*Psalm 126:5*

May your unfailing love be my comfort, according to your promise to your servant.

—*Psalm 119:76*

Even though I walk through the valley of the shadow of death, I will fear no evil, for you are with me; your rod and your staff, they comfort me.

—*Psalm 23:4*

Jesus said: "I will not leave you as orphans; I will come to you."

—John 14:18

Praise be to the God and Father of our Lord Jesus Christ, the Father of compassion and the God of all comfort, who comforts us in all our troubles, so that we can comfort those in any trouble with the comfort we ourselves have received from God. For just as the sufferings of Christ flow over into our lives, so also through Christ our comfort overflows.

—2 Corinthians 1:3-5

Cast all your anxiety on him because he cares for you.

—1 Peter 5:7

The righteous cry out, and the LORD hears them; he delivers them from all their troubles. The LORD is close to the brokenhearted and saves those who are crushed in spirit

—*Psalm 34:17-18*

So do not fear, for I am with you; do not be dismayed, for I am your God. I will strengthen you and help you; I will uphold you with my righteous right hand.

—*Isaiah 41:10*

Be strong and courageous. Do not be afraid or terrified because of them, for the LORD your God goes with you; he will never leave you nor forsake you.

—*Deuteronomy 31:6*

I will turn their mourning into gladness; I will give them comfort and joy instead of sorrow.

—*Jeremiah 31:13*

The LORD is gracious and righteous; our God is full of compassion.

—*Psalm 116:5*

The salvation of the righteous comes from the LORD; he is their stronghold in time of trouble.

—*Psalm 37:39*

Creation

The LORD is good to all; he has compassion on all he has made. All you have made will praise you, O LORD; your saints will extol you.

—*Psalm 145:9-10*

Blessed be your glorious name, [LORD], and may it be exalted above all blessing and praise. You alone are the LORD. You made the heavens, even the highest heavens, and all their starry host, the earth and all that is on it, the seas and all that is in them. You give life to everything, and the multitudes of heaven worship you.

—*Nehemiah 9:5-6*

Praise him, sun and moon, praise him, all you shining stars. Praise him, you highest heavens and you waters above the skies. Let them praise the name of the LORD, for he commanded and they were created. He set them in place for ever and ever; he gave a decree that will never pass away. Praise the LORD from the earth, you great sea creatures and all ocean depths, lightning and hail, snow and clouds, stormy winds that do his bidding, you mountains and all hills, fruit trees and all cedars, wild animals and all cattle, small creatures and flying birds.

—*Psalm 148:3-10*

He alone stretches out the heavens and treads on the waves of the sea. He is the Maker of the Bear and Orion, the Pleiades and the constellations of the south. He performs wonders that cannot be fathomed, miracles that cannot be counted.

—*Job 9:8-10*

Praise the LORD, O my soul. O LORD my God, you are very great; you are clothed with splendor and majesty. He wraps himself in light as with a garment; he stretches out the heavens like a tent and lays the beams of his upper chambers on their waters. He makes the clouds his chariot and rides on the wings of the wind. He makes winds his messengers, flames of fire his servants.

—*Psalm 104:1-4*

When you send your Spirit, they are created, and you renew the face of the earth.

—Psalm 104:30

The world is firmly established; it cannot be moved. Let the heavens rejoice, let the earth be glad; let them say among the nations, "The LORD reigns!" Let the sea resound, and all that is in it; let the fields be jubilant, and everything in them! Then the trees of the forest will sing, they will sing for joy before the LORD, for he comes to judge the earth. Give thanks to the LORD, for he is good; his love endures forever.

—1 Chronicles 16:30-34

When I consider your heavens, the work of your fingers, the moon and the stars, which you have set in place, what is man that you are mindful of him, the son of man that you care for him? You made him a little lower than the heavenly beings and crowned him with glory and honor.

—Psalm 8:3-5

How many are your works, O Lord! In wisdom you made them all; the earth is full of your creatures. There is the sea, vast and spacious, teeming with creatures beyond number–living things both large and small.

—Psalm 104:24-25

Guidance

Good and upright is the LORD; therefore he instructs sinners in his ways. He guides the humble in what is right and teaches them his way.

—*Psalm 25:8-9*

Where can I go from your Spirit? Where can I flee from your presence? If I rise on the wings of the dawn, if I settle on the far side of the sea, even there your hand will guide me, your right hand will hold me fast.

—*Psalm 139:7,9-10*

This God is our God for ever and ever; he will be our guide even to the end.

—*Psalm 48:14*

Trust in the LORD with all your heart and lean not on your own understanding; in all your ways acknowledge him, and he will make your paths straight.

—*Proverbs 3:5-6*

May the peoples praise you, O God; may all the peoples praise you. May the nations be glad and sing for joy, for you rule the peoples justly and guide the nations of the earth.

—*Psalm 67:3-4*

Peace

Jesus said: "Peace I leave with you; my peace I give you. I do not give to you as the world gives. Do not let your hearts be troubled and do not be afraid."

—*John 14:27*

Since we have been justified through faith, we have peace with God through our Lord Jesus Christ.

—*Romans 5:1*

The wisdom that comes from heaven is first of all pure; then peace-loving, considerate, submissive, full of mercy and good fruit, impartial and sincere. Peacemakers who sow in peace raise a harvest of righteousness.

—*James 3:17-18*

I will lie down and sleep in peace, for you alone, O LORD, make me dwell in safety.

—*Psalm 4:8*

I will heal my people and will let them enjoy abundant peace and security.

—*Jeremiah 33:6*

Grace and peace be yours in abundance through the knowledge of God and of Jesus our Lord.

—*2 Peter 1:2*

"I know the plans I have for you," declares the LORD, "plans to prosper you and not to harm you, plans to give you hope and a future."

—*Jeremiah 29:11*

The kingdom of God is not a matter of eating and drinking, but of righteousness, peace and joy in the Holy Spirit.

—*Romans 14:17*

I will listen to what God the LORD will say; he promises peace to his people, his saints.

—*Psalm 85:8*

Aim for perfection, be of one mind, live in peace. And the God of love and peace will be with you.

—*2 Corinthians 13:11*

He grants peace to your borders and satisfies you with the finest of wheat.

—*Psalm 147:14*

For to us a child is born, to us a son is given, and the government will be on his shoulders. And he will be called Wonderful Counselor, Mighty God, Everlasting Father, Prince of Peace.

—*Isaiah 9:6*

Jesus said: "I have told you these things, so that in me you may have peace. In this world you will have trouble. But take heart! I have overcome the world."

—*John 16:33*

The peace of God, which transcends all understanding, will guard your hearts and your minds in Christ Jesus.

—*Philippians 4:7*

Presence of the Holy Spirit

The disciples were filled with joy and with the Holy Spirit.

—*Acts 13:52*

May the God of hope fill you with all joy and peace as you trust in him, so that you may overflow with hope by the power of the Holy Spirit.

—*Romans 15:13*

Blessed are those who have learned to acclaim you, who walk in the light of your presence, O LORD.

—*Psalm 89:15*

You have made known to me the paths of life; you will fill me with joy in your presence.

—*Acts 2:28*

Repent and be baptized, every one of you, in the name of Jesus Christ for the forgiveness of your sins. And you will receive the gift of the Holy Spirit.

—*Acts 2:38*

Jesus told his disciples, "The Counselor, the Holy Spirit, whom the Father will send in my name, will teach you all things and will remind you of everything I have said to you."

—*John 14:26*

Be filled with the Spirit.

—*Ephesians 5:18*

The LORD said: "My Presence will go with you, and I will give you rest."

—*Exodus 33:14*

Those who belong to Christ Jesus have crucified the sinful nature with its passions and desires. Since we live by the Spirit, let us keep in step with the Spirit.

—*Galatians 5:24-25*

If you then, though you are evil, know how to give good gifts to your children, how much more will your Father in heaven give the Holy Spirit to those who ask him!

—*Luke 11:13*

Protection & Provision

As for God, his way is perfect; the word of the LORD is flawless. He is a shield for all who take refuge in him.

—2 Samuel 22:31

You are my hiding place; you will protect me from trouble and surround me with songs of deliverance.

—Psalm 32:7

The LORD is my rock, my fortress and my deliverer; my God is my rock, in whom I take refuge, my shield and the horn of my salvation. He is my stronghold, my refuge and my savior … I call to the LORD, who is worthy of praise, and I am saved from my enemies.

—2 Samuel 22:2-4

When you have eaten and are satisfied, praise the LORD your God for the good land he has given you.

—*Deuteronomy 8:10*

The poor will eat and be satisfied; they who seek the LORD will praise him.

—*Psalm 22:26*

The cords of death entangled me; the torrents of destruction overwhelmed me. The cords of the grave coiled around me; the snares of death confronted me. In my distress I called to the LORD; I cried to my God for help. From his temple he heard my voice; my cry came before him, into his ears.

—*Psalm 18:4-6*

You will have plenty to eat, until you are full, and you will praise the name of the LORD your God, who has worked wonders for you.

—*Joel 2:26*

He holds victory in store for the upright, he is a shield to those whose walk is blameless, for he guards the course of the just and protects the way of his faithful ones.

—*Proverbs 2:7-8*

The angel of the LORD encamps around those who fear him, and he delivers them.

—*Psalm 34:7*

Cast your cares on the LORD and he will sustain you; he will never let the righteous fall.

—*Psalm 55:22*

May the LORD answer you when you are in distress; may the name of the God of Jacob protect you. May he send you help from the sanctuary and grant you support from Zion … May he give you the desire of your heart and make all your plans succeed. We will shout for joy when you are victorious and will lift up our banners in the name of our God. May the LORD grant all your requests. Now I know that the LORD saves his anointed; he answers him from his holy heaven with the saving power of his right hand. Some trust in chariots and some in horses, but we trust in the name of the LORD our God.

—*Psalm 20:1-2, 4-7*

Fulfill your vows to the Most High, and call upon me in the day of trouble; I will deliver you, and you will honor me.

—*Psalm 50:14-15*

The LORD is good, a refuge in times of trouble. He cares for those who trust in him.

—*Nahum 1:7*

Salvation

Whoever hears my word and believes him who sent me has eternal life and will not be condemned; he has crossed over from death to life.

—*John 5:24*

The LORD is my strength and my song; he has become my salvation. He is my God, and I will praise him, my father's God, and I will exalt him.

—*Exodus 15:2*

I delight greatly in the LORD; my soul rejoices in my God. For he has clothed me with garments of salvation and arrayed me in a robe of righteousness, as a bridegroom adorns his head like a priest, and as a bride adorns herself with her jewels.

—*Isaiah 61:10*

Why are you downcast, O my soul? Why so disturbed within me? Put your hope in God, for I will yet praise him, my Savior and my God.

—*Psalm 42:5-6*

My soul finds rest in God alone; my salvation comes from him. He alone is my rock and my salvation; he is my fortress, I will never be shaken.

—*Psalm 62:1-2*

Sing to the LORD a new song, for he has done marvelous things; his right hand and his holy arm have worked salvation for him. The LORD has made his salvation known and revealed his righteousness to the nations.

—*Psalm 98:1-2*

Surely this is our God; we trusted in him, and he saved us. This is the LORD, we trusted in him; let us rejoice and be glad in his salvation.

—*Isaiah 25:9*

Christ was sacrificed once to take away the sins of many people; and he will appear a second time, not to bear sin, but to bring salvation to those who are waiting for him.

—*Hebrews 9:28*

Jesus said: "Whoever drinks the water I give him will never thirst. Indeed, the water I give him will become in him a spring of water welling up to eternal life."

—*John 4:14*

Godly sorrow brings repentance that leads to salvation and leaves no regret.

—*2 Corinthians 7:10*

May all who seek you rejoice and be glad in you; may those who love your salvation always say, "The LORD be exalted!"

—*Psalm 40:16*

With joy you will draw water from the wells of salvation.

—*Isaiah 12:3*

I was shown mercy so that in me, the worst of sinners, Christ Jesus might display his unlimited patience as an example for those who would believe on him and receive eternal life.

—*1 Timothy 1:16*

Sing to the LORD, all the earth; proclaim his salvation day after day.

—*1 Chronicles 16:23*

Jesus said: "My sheep listen to my voice; I know them, and they follow me. I give them eternal life, and they shall never perish; no one can snatch them out of my hand."

—*John 10:27-28*

If you confess with your mouth, "Jesus is Lord," and believe in your heart that God raised him from the dead, you will be saved.

—*Romans 10:9*

A Simple Way of *Worshiping*

Praise the L*ORD.*
Sing to the L*ORD a new song, his praise in the assembly of the saints.*

—2 CHRONICLES 7:6

Praising God's Very Nature

Stand up and praise the LORD your God, who is from everlasting to everlasting: Blessed be your glorious name, and may it be exalted above all blessing and praise. You alone are the LORD. You made the heavens, even the highest heavens, and all their starry host, the earth and all that is on it, the seas and all that is in them. You give life to everything, and the multitudes of heaven worship you.

—Nehemiah 9:5-6

Ascribe to the LORD the glory due his name; worship the LORD in the splendor of his holiness.

—Psalm 29:2

I lift up my eyes to you, to you whose throne is in heaven.

—*Psalm 123:1*

Do you not know? Have you not heard? The LORD is the everlasting God, the Creator of the ends of the earth. He will not grow tired or weary, and his understanding no one can fathom. He gives strength to the weary and increases the power of the weak. Even youths grow tired and weary, and young men stumble and fall; but those who hope in the LORD will renew their strength. They will soar on wings like eagles; they will run and not grow weary, they will walk and not be faint.

—*Isaiah 40:28-31*

God said, "I desire mercy, not sacrifice, and acknowledgment of God rather than burnt offerings."

—*Leviticus 26:2*

I know that the LORD is great, that our Lord is greater than all gods.

—*Psalm 135:5*

Celebrating God's Goodness

Great is the LORD and most worthy of praise; his greatness no one can fathom. One generation will commend your works to another; they will tell of your mighty acts. They will speak of the glorious splendor of your majesty, and I will meditate on your wonderful works. They will tell of the power of your awesome works, and I will proclaim your great deeds. They will celebrate your abundant goodness and joyfully sing of your righteousness.

—*Psalm 145:3-7*

May your saints rejoice in your goodness.

—*2 Chronicles 6:41*

The Lord is good, a refuge in times of trouble. He cares for those who trust in him.

—Psalm 34:8

Worship the LORD with gladness; come before him with joyful songs. Know that the LORD is God. It is he who made us, and we are his; we are his people, the sheep of his pasture. Enter his gates with thanksgiving and his courts with praise; give thanks to him and praise his name. For the LORD is good and his love endures forever; his faithfulness continues through all generations.

—Psalm 100:2-5

How can I repay the LORD for all his goodness to me?

—Psalm 116:12

For you who revere God's name, the sun of righteousness will rise with healing in its wings. And you will go out and leap like calves released from the stall.

—Malachi 4:2

The trumpeters and singers joined in unison, as with one voice, to give praise and thanks to the Lord. Accompanied by trumpets, cymbals and other instruments, they raised their voices in praise to the Lord and sang: "He is good; his love endures forever."

—2 Chronicles 5:13

I am still confident of this: I will see the goodness of the LORD in the land of the living.

—Psalm 27:13

Worshiping Together

Come, let us bow down in worship, let us kneel before the LORD our Maker; for he is our God and we are the people of his pasture, the flock under his care.

—*Psalm 95:6-7*

The priests took their positions, as did the Levites with the Lord's musical instruments, which King David had made for praising the Lord and which were used when he gave thanks, saying, "His love endures forever." Opposite the Levites, the priests blew their trumpets, and all the Israelites were standing.

—*John 12:12-13*

Worshiping Together

Glorify the LORD with me; let us exalt his name together.

—Psalm 34:3

I will give you thanks in the great assembly; among throngs of people I will praise you.

—1 Chronicles 29:20

Exalting God

Be still, and know that I am God; I will be exalted among the nations, I will be exalted in the earth.

—Psalm 46:10

Know therefore that the LORD your God is God; he is the faithful God, keeping his covenant of love to a thousand generations of those who love him and keep his commands.

—Deuteronomy 7:9

Since we are receiving a kingdom that cannot be shaken, let us be thankful, and so worship God acceptably with reverence and awe.

—Hebrews 12:28

The prophet Elijah stepped forward and prayed: "O LORD, God of Abraham, Isaac and Israel, let it be known today that you are God in Israel and that I am your servant and have done all these things at your command. Answer me, O LORD, answer me, so these people will know that you, O LORD, are God, and that you are turning their hearts back again."

—*1 Kings 18:36-37*

God said, "I desire mercy, not sacrifice, and acknowledgment of God rather than burnt offerings."

—*Leviticus 26:2*

Know that the LORD is God. It is he who made us, and we are his; we are his people, the sheep of his pasture.

—*Psalm 100:3*

It is the LORD your God you must follow, and him you must revere. Keep his commands and obey him; serve him and hold fast to him.

—Deuteronomy 13:4

I will give them a heart to know me, that I am the LORD. They will be my people, and I will be their God, for they will return to me with all their heart.

—Jeremiah 24:7

God Is With Us

The LORD your God is with you, he is mighty to save. He will take great delight in you, he will quiet you with his love, he will rejoice over you with singing.

—*Zephaniah 3:17*

The LORD is with me; I will not be afraid. What can man do to me? The LORD is with me; he is my helper. I will look in triumph on my enemies.

—*Psalm 118:6-7*

God said to Jacob: "I am with you and will watch over you wherever you go, and I will bring you back to this land. I will not leave you until I have done what I have promised you."

—*Genesis 28:15*

Do not fear, for I am with you; do not be dismayed, for I am your God. I will strengthen you and help you; I will uphold you with my righteous right hand.

—Isaiah 41:10

Surely, Lord, you have granted me eternal blessings and made me glad with the joy of your presence.

—Psalm 21:6

In my integrity you uphold me and set me in your presence forever. Praise be to the Lord, the God of Israel, from everlasting to everlasting. Amen and Amen.

—Psalm 41:12-13

David said to Solomon his son, "Be strong and courageous, and do the work. Do not be afraid or discouraged, for the LORD God, my God, is with you. He will not fail you or forsake you until all the work for the service of the temple of the LORD is finished."

—*1 Chronicles 28:20*

The LORD replied, "My Presence will go with you, and I will give you rest."

—*Exodus 33:14*

Haggai, the LORD'S messenger, gave this message of the LORD to the people: " 'I am with you,' declares the LORD."

—*Haggai 1:13*

Jesus said, "Go and make disciples of all nations, baptizing them in the name of the Father and of the Son and of the Holy Spirit, and teaching them to obey everything I have commanded you. And surely I am with you always, to the very end of the age."

—*Matthew 28:19-20*

Blessed are those who have learned to acclaim you, who walk in the light of your presence, O LORD. They rejoice in your name all day long; they exult in your righteousness. For you are their glory and strength. Indeed, our shield belongs to the LORD, our king to the Holy One of Israel.

—*Psalm 89:15-18*

Jesus' Example

Jesus answered, "It is written: 'Worship the Lord your God and serve him only.' "

—Luke 4:8

Jesus looked toward heaven and prayed: "Father, the time has come. Glorify your Son, that your Son may glorify you. For you granted him authority over all people that he might give eternal life to all those you have given him. Now this is eternal life: that they may know you, the only true God, and Jesus Christ, whom you have sent."

—John 17:1-3

Jesus said, "Yet a time is coming and has now come when the true worshipers will worship the Father in spirit and truth, for they are the kind of worshipers the Father seeks."

—*John 4:23*

Examples of *Worship*

Give thanks to the LORD*, for he is good. His love endures forever.*

PSALM 136:1

Angels

Suddenly a great company of the heavenly host appeared with the angel, praising God and saying, "Glory to God in the highest."

—Luke 2:13-14

I looked and heard the voice of many angels, numbering thousands upon thousands, and ten thousand times ten thousand. They encircled the throne and the living creatures and the elders. In a loud voice they sang: "Worthy is the Lamb, who was slain, to receive power and wealth and wisdom and strength and honor and glory and praise!"

— Revelation 5:11-12

All the angels were standing around the throne and around the elders and the four living creatures. They fell down on their faces before the throne and worshiped God, saying: "Amen! Praise and glory and wisdom and thanks and honor and power and strength be to our God for ever and ever. Amen!"

—*Revelation 7:11-12*

Praise the LORD, you his angels, you mighty ones who do his bidding, who obey his word. Praise the LORD, all his heavenly hosts, you his servants who do his will.

—*Psalm 103:20-21*

When God brings his firstborn into the world, he says, "Let all God's angels worship him."

—*Hebrews 1:6*

Praise the LORD. Praise the LORD from the heavens, praise him in the heights above. Praise him, all his angels, praise him, all his heavenly hosts.

—*Psalm 148:1-2*

Daniel

Daniel praised the God of heaven and said: "Praise be to the name of God for ever and ever; wisdom and power are his. He changes times and seasons; he sets up kings and deposes them. He gives wisdom to the wise and knowledge to the discerning. He reveals deep and hidden things; he knows what lies in darkness, and light dwells with him. I thank and praise you, O God of my fathers: You have given me wisdom and power, you have made known to me what we asked of you, you have made known to us the dream of the king."

—*Daniel 2:19-23*

David

Give thanks to the LORD, for he is
good. *His love endures forever.*
Give thanks to the God of gods.
His love endures forever.
Give thanks to the LORD of lords:
His love endures forever.
to him who alone does great wonders, *His love endures forever.*
who by his understanding made
the heavens,
His love endures forever.
who spread out the earth upon the
waters, *His love endures forever.*
who made the great lights—
His love endures forever.
the sun to govern the day,
His love endures forever.
the moon and stars to govern the
night; *His love endures forever.*

to the One who remembered us in
our low estate
His love endures forever.
and freed us from our enemies,
His love endures forever.
and who gives food to every creature.
His love endures forever.
Give thanks to the God of heaven.
His love endures forever.

—*Psalm 136:1-9,23-26*

Deborah and Barak

Deborah and Barak son of Abinoam sang this song:

"When the princes in Israel take the lead, when the people willingly offer themselves—praise the LORD!

"Hear this, you kings! Listen, you rulers! I will sing to the LORD, I will sing; I will make music to the LORD, the God of Israel.

"O LORD, when you went out from Seir, when you marched from the land of Edom, the earth shook, the heavens poured, the clouds poured down water. The mountains quaked before the LORD, the One of Sinai, before the LORD, the God of Israel.

"In the days of Shamgar son of Anath, in the days of Jael, the roads were abandoned; travelers took to winding paths. Village life in Israel ceased, ceased until I, Deborah, arose, arose a mother in Israel. When they chose new gods, war came to the city gates, and not a shield or spear was seen among forty thousand in Israel. My heart is with Israel's princes, with the willing volunteers among the people. Praise the LORD!

"You who ride on white donkeys, sitting on your saddle blankets, and you who walk along the road, consider the voice of the singers at the watering places. They recite the righteous acts of the LORD, the righteous acts of his warriors in Israel.

"Then the people of the LORD went down to the city gates. 'Wake up, wake up, Deborah! Wake up, wake up, break out in song! Arise, O Barak! Take captive your captives, O son of Abinoam.'

"So may all your enemies perish, O LORD! But may they who love you be like the sun when it rises in its strength."

—*Judges 5:1-12,31*

Hannah

Hannah prayed and said:

"My heart rejoices in the LORD; in the LORD my horn is lifted high. My mouth boasts over my enemies, for I delight in your deliverance.

"There is no one holy like the LORD; there is no one besides you; there is no Rock like our God.

"The LORD sends poverty and wealth; he humbles and he exalts. He raises the poor from the dust and lifts the needy from the ash heap; he seats them with princes and has them inherit a throne of honor.

"For the foundations of the earth are the LORD's; upon them he has set the world. He will guard the feet of his saints."

—1 Samuel 2:1-2,7-9

Mary

Mary said:

"My soul glorifies the Lord and my spirit rejoices in God my Savior, for he has been mindful of the humble state of his servant. From now on all generations will call me blessed, for the Mighty One has done great things for me—holy is his name. His mercy extends to those who fear him, from generation to generation. He has performed mighty deeds with his arm; he has scattered those who are proud in their inmost thoughts. He has brought down rulers from their thrones but has lifted up the humble. He has filled the hungry with good things but has sent the rich away empty. He has helped his servant Israel, remembering to be merciful to Abraham and his descendants forever, even as he said to our fathers."

—*Luke 1:46-55*

Moses

Moses and the Israelites sang this song to the LORD:

"I will sing to the LORD, for he is highly exalted. The horse and its rider he has hurled into the sea. The LORD is my strength and my song; he has become my salvation. He is my God, and I will praise him, my father's God, and I will exalt him. The LORD is a warrior; the LORD is his name. Pharaoh's chariots and his army he has hurled into the sea. The best of Pharaoh's officers are drowned in the Red Sea. The deep waters have covered them; they sank to the depths like a stone.

"Your right hand, O LORD, was majestic in power. Your right hand, O LORD, shattered the enemy.

"Who among the gods is like you, O LORD? Who is like you—majestic in holiness, awesome in glory, working wonders? You stretched out your right hand and the earth swallowed them.

"In your unfailing love you will lead the people you have redeemed. In your strength you will guide them to your holy dwelling.

"You will bring them in and plant them on the mountain of your inheritance—the place, O LORD, you made for your dwelling, the sanctuary, O LORD, your hands established. The LORD will reign for ever and ever."

—*Exodus 15:1-6,11-13,17-18*

Simeon

Now there was a man in Jerusalem called Simeon, who was righteous and devout. He was waiting for the consolation of Israel, and the Holy Spirit was upon him. It had been revealed to him by the Holy Spirit that he would not die before he had seen the Lord's Christ. Moved by the Spirit, he went into the temple courts. When the parents brought in the child Jesus to do for him what the custom of the Law required, Simeon took him in his arms and praised God, saying:

"Sovereign Lord, as you have promised, you now dismiss your servant in peace. For my eyes have seen your salvation, which you have prepared in the sight of all people, a light for revelation to the Gentiles and for glory to your people Israel."

—*Luke 2:25-32*

Solomon

Solomon said:

"Praise be to the LORD, the God of Israel, who with his hands has fulfilled what he promised with his mouth to my father David. For he said, 'Since the day I brought my people out of Egypt, I have not chosen a city in any tribe of Israel to have a temple built for my Name to be there, nor have I chosen anyone to be the leader over my people Israel. But now I have chosen Jerusalem for my Name to be there, and I have chosen David to rule my people Israel.'

"My father David had it in his heart to build a temple for the Name of the LORD, the God of Israel. But the LORD said to my father David, 'Because it was in your heart to build a temple for my Name, you did well to have this in your heart. Nevertheless, you are not the one to build the temple, but your son, who is your own flesh and blood—he is the one who will build the temple for my Name.'

"The LORD has kept the promise he made. I have succeeded David my father and now I sit on the throne of Israel, just as the LORD promised, and I have built the temple for the Name of the LORD, the God of Israel. There I have placed the ark, in which is the covenant of the LORD that he made with the people of Israel.

"O LORD, God of Israel, there is no God like you in heaven or on earth—you who keep your covenant of love with your servants who continue wholeheartedly in your way. You have kept your promise to your servant David my father; with your mouth you have promised and with your hand you have fulfilled it—as it is today."

—*2 Chronicles 6:4-11,14-15*

Zechariah

Zechariah was filled with the Holy Spirit and prophesied:

"Praise be to the Lord, the God of Israel, because he has come and has redeemed his people. He has raised up a horn of salvation for us in the house of his servant David (as he said through his holy prophets of long ago), salvation from our enemies and from the hand of all who hate us—to show mercy to our fathers and to remember his holy covenant, the oath he swore to our father Abraham: to rescue us from the hand of our enemies, and to enable us to serve him without fear in holiness and righteousness before him all our days.

"And you, my child, will be called a prophet of the Most High; for you will go on before the Lord to prepare the way for him, to give his people the knowledge of salvation through the forgiveness of their sins, because of the tender mercy of our God, by which the rising sun will come to us from heaven to shine on those living in darkness and in the shadow of death, to guide our feet into the path of peace."

—*Luke 1:67-79*